HISTORY HUNTERS

FROZEN MAMMOTH

by Dougal Dixon

Gareth Stevens Publishing
A WORLD ALMANAC EDUCATION GROUP COMPANY

Please visit our web site at: www.garethstevens.com
For a free color catalog describing Gareth Stevens Publishing's
list of high-quality books and multimedia programs,
call 1-800-542-2595 (USA) or 1-800-387-3178 (Canada).
Gareth Stevens Publishing's fax: (414) 332-3567.

Library of Congress Cataloging-in-Publication Data

Dixon, Dougal.
    Frozen mammoth / by Dougal Dixon. — North American ed.
      p. cm. — (History hunters)
    Summary: Describes an expedition to uncover and study a frozen mammoth in Siberia.
    Includes bibliographical references and index.
    ISBN 0-8368-3740-1 (lib. bdg.)
    1. Mammoths—Russia (Federation)—Siberia—Juvenile literature. 2. Glacial epoch—Russia
(Federation)—Siberia—Juvenile literature. [1. Mammoths. 2. Glacial epoch. 3. Excavations
(Archaeology).] I. Title. II. Series.
    QE882.P8D89   2003
    569'.67—dc21   2003045717

This North American edition first published in 2004 by
Gareth Stevens Publishing
A World Almanac Education Group Company
330 West Olive Street, Suite 100
Milwaukee, WI 53212 USA

This U.S. edition copyright © 2004 by Gareth Stevens, Inc. Original edition copyright © 2003 ticktock
Entertainment Ltd. First published in Great Britain in 2003 by ticktock Media Ltd., Unit 2, Orchard Business
Centre, North Farm Road, Tunbridge Wells, Kent, TN2 3XF. Additional end matter copyright © 2004 by
Gareth Stevens, Inc.

We would like to thank: David Gillingwater, Dr. Adrian Lister, and Elizabeth Wiggans.

Illustrations by John Alston and Simon Mendez.

Gareth Stevens editor: Carol Ryback
Gareth Stevens cover design: Katherine A. Goedheer

Photo credits:
t=top, b=bottom, c=center, l=left, r=right, OFC=outside front cover, OBC=outside back cover

Agence France Presse: 22b. Alamy images: 3br, 3bl, 4cr, 4br, 6tr, 8bl, 12-13, 12tr, 13br, 14b, 15tr,
15c, 19tr, 20-21c, 21tr, 23c. John Alston: 7tr, 7cr, 7cl, 7tl, 8cr. Ancient Art & Architecture Collection
Ltd 27. Corbis: 4bc, 7bl, 11tl, 12br, 13cr, 14-15c, 16-17c, 17tr, 27br, 29. Natural History Museum:
15br. Science Photo Library: 4bl, 11tr, 18b, 19c. Simon Mendez: 8tr, 9tl, 9tr. Topham Picturepoint:
23tl. Torquay Museum: 10tl, 10br, 11b.

Printed in Hong Kong

1 2 3 4 5 6 7 8 9 07 06 05 04 03

Would you like to join an expedition to hunt for a frozen mammoth?

The characters accompanying you — Charlie Smith, Dr. Marilyn Petronella, Max J. Heidelmann III, and the crew from the Boffinbox Science Channel — are fictitious, but the facts about museums, paleontologists, and scientists represent an accurate view of their work. The frozen mammoth you are about to discover is also fictitious, but the characteristics and details of its life are based on facts about other discoveries of woolly mammoths.

Can't wait to learn more? Ready to dig for ancient clues?
Then welcome to the City Museum...

CONTENTS

CITY MUSEUM PASS

Name: Dr. Marilyn Petronella
Position: Curator
Department: Paleontology

Interests: Mammoths, dinosaurs, digging, and rock climbing.

CITY MUSEUM PASS

Name: Charlie Smith
Postion: Research Assistant
Department: Paleontology

Interests: Mammoths, dinosaurs, and skateboarding.

TEMPORARY

AN EXCITING DAY

Siberia is the northernmost section of the huge Russian Federation.

Day 1

I have always loved visiting the City Museum with its huge collection of fascinating items from around the world, and now I have a temporary job in the museum's storeroom. I'm sorting artifacts from an expedition to Siberia.

The museum's ethnographer – someone who studies different groups of people around the world – traveled to Siberia to study reindeer-herding tribes. Expedition items include an odd-shaped tooth and a shriveled up piece of skin attached to some hair. I think both artifacts came from a mammoth.

Only a few completely frozen and preserved mammoths have been found, but some experts think up to ten million of these animals are buried in areas close to the Arctic Circle. Right now, a City Museum expedition crew is back in Siberia looking for another mammoth. I'd love to join the search!

Ural Mountains

A woman from the Nenet people feeds some of her reindeer. The Nenet create elaborate carvings from reindeer antlers.

Herders from the Yamal Peninsula in Siberia carved this traditional Nenet knife from a reindeer antler.

The smaller size of this mammoth tooth indicates that it came from a young animal.

We must determine if this piece of skin and bone is from a woolly mammoth.

I've marked where some of the Siberian mammoths were found.

Arctic Ocean

The last mammoth to leave Russia permanently was excavated in 1901-1903 from the Liakhov Islands and sent to Paris, France.

1901 – Kolyma River: The Beresovka Mammoth is now on display in the St. Petersburg Museum.

A french-led international team extracted the Jarkov mammoth from the Taimyr Peninsula in 1999.

Mascha, a baby mammoth, was found on the Yaml Peninsula in 1988.

In 1977, gold miners in Berelekh found a baby mammoth, nicknamed Dima.

The City Museum's mammoth remains were found somewhere in this area. A local gold miner told us that both pieces came from a frozen riverbank.

Khatanga – a former nickel mine now functions as a study center and provides cold storage for the mammoth remains.

The Lena River Delta is where Mikhail Adams discovered the first frozen mammoth in 1806.

Central Siberian Plain

Reindeer herders decorate belts with glass beads.

From: City Museum Ethnography Department
To: Charlie Smith
Subject: Siberian Expedition

Dear Charlie,

A few years back, some of us studied the Siberian reindeer herders and collected some of their traditional handicrafts. Siberia is the northernmost part of the Russian Federation. During the twentieth century, the Soviet Union officials persuaded the reindeer herders to leave their traditional lands to work in the cities. After the Soviet Union broke up in the early 1990s, the herders returned to their old ways of life. Our team wanted to learn how the tribes were going about rebuilding their traditions — a very important part of ethnography. While we were on the banks of the Yenisei River, a local man gave us the mammoth artifacts you mentioned in your note to us. Please show them to Dr. Marilyn Petronella, the City Museum's Curator of Paleontology. I'm sure she can help you with further research on woolly mammoths.

USER 1
USER 2
USER 3

Day 2

Dr. Marilyn Petronella, the City Museum's chief paleontologist, is very excited about the mammoth remains I found in our storeroom. She says that mammoths are extinct members of the elephant family. I've done some research ranging from the earliest known elephants to the two species alive today. Mammoths lived from about four million years ago until just a few thousand years ago. The most recent species was a dwarf form that lived about 3,700 years ago and was discovered in 1992. The dwarf mammoths lived on Wrangel Island off the northeast coast of Siberia and were about 6 feet (2 meters) tall. Species that evolve on islands are often smaller in size because of limited food supplies.

Dr. Petronella thinks that our tooth came from a young animal of a larger mammoth species. She is certain the hair and bone came from an adult animal. Maybe we will find a whole herd of frozen mammoths!

An Asian elephant is often trained to work. Mammoths had the same basic shape as modern elephants but with sloping backs, curved and twisted tusks, and shaggy hair.

Ponies from the Scottish Shetland Islands are a modern example of dwarf animals living on islands.

SHETLAND PONIES

Early members of the mammal group Proboscidea. Modern elephants are the latest-evolving example.

1. MOERITHERIUM

Moeritherium, the earliest known proboscidean, lived during the Eocene epoch about fifty million years ago. It was about the size of a tapir. It had no trunk or tusks.

2. PHIOMIA

By the Oligocene epoch, thirty million years ago, proboscideans had become larger — 8 feet (2.5 m) high at the shoulder. They were beginning to develop tusks and a trunk to help them feed.

3. GOMPHOTHERIUM

Gompotherium lived ten million years ago, in the Miocene epoch. They had tusks in their upper jaw and in their very long lower jaw. They had fewer chewing teeth than their ancestors, but their teeth were larger.

4. DEINOTHERIUM

Deinotherium lived from ten million to one million years ago, during the Miocene to Pleistocene epochs. Its only tusks curved downward from its lower jaw. The tusks were probably used as picks for digging.

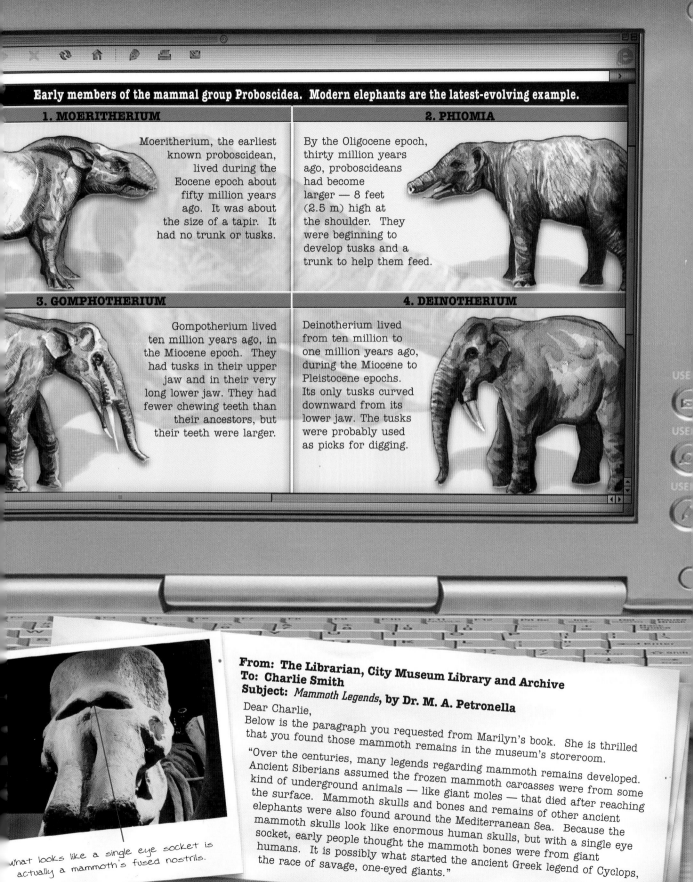

What looks like a single eye socket is actually a mammoth's fused nostrils.

From: The Librarian, City Museum Library and Archive
To: Charlie Smith
Subject: *Mammoth Legends*, by Dr. M. A. Petronella

Dear Charlie,

Below is the paragraph you requested from Marilyn's book. She is thrilled that you found those mammoth remains in the museum's storeroom.

"Over the centuries, many legends regarding mammoth remains developed. Ancient Siberians assumed the frozen mammoth carcasses were from some kind of underground animals — like giant moles — that died after reaching the surface. Mammoth skulls and bones and remains of other ancient elephants were also found around the Mediterranean Sea. Because the mammoth skulls look like enormous human skulls, but with a single eye socket, early people thought the mammoth bones were from giant humans. It is possibly what started the ancient Greek legend of Cyclops, the race of savage, one-eyed giants."

THE PAST PRESERVED

Day 3

I'm learning so much about frozen mammoths that Dr. Petronella wants me to display my research for other kids my age!

I always thought mammoths were frozen in ice, but they were really preserved by frozen mud. Mammoths lived during the Ice Ages (about one million to 10,000 years ago) in the cold, dry climate in northern Asia. They lived in open, rolling grassland areas called tundra. Mucky, black soil overlaid the permafrost (a permanently frozen, subsurface soil layer).

Most preserved mammoths come from two time periods — either before 30,000 years ago or between 13,000 and 10,000 years ago — when a somewhat mild climate made the permafrost unstable. A mammoth weighing three tons could easily get trapped and sink in a thawed, boggy area. When the bog froze again, it acted like a giant deep-freeze that preserved the dead mammoth.

FROZEN CHICKEN

1. Mammoths roamed the tundra in herds. They used their trunks to pull up low vegetation and grass.

Mudflow

Frozen mud

Northern Siberia now consists of tundra (boggy ground with little vegetation). In the mammoths' time it would have been cold grassland.

Ice Age Mammoths

2. When the weather became milder, the underlying permafrost thawed out and formed deep, boggy patches that could trap the heavy mammoths.

3. Trapped mammoths drowned or suffocated. Dense mud preserved the bodies until the ground holding them froze solid.

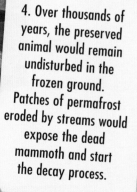

4. Over thousands of years, the preserved animal would remain undisturbed in the frozen ground. Patches of permafrost eroded by streams would expose the dead mammoth and start the decay process.

DON'T FORGET THE CHICKEN!

From: Dr. Marilyn Petronella
To: Charlie Smith, The City Museum
Subject: Defrosting mammoths

Dear Charlie,
I hope you aren't going to work too late — after all, it's Friday night. By the way, did I leave my frozen chicken in the office? It will thaw out now and be spoiled by Monday. No Sunday lunch for me! That's exactly what happens to a frozen mammoth if it is exposed to the air for too long — it thaws, rots away, and is useless for study. I've been thinking, we better find our frozen mammoth before it thaws out and goes bad! I will contact the experts in the mammoth department of the Museum of Zoology in St. Petersburg, Russia. I'll let them know about our plans for a frozen-mammoth-hunting expedition. They may help us. I want you to join the expedition, especially since you were the one who found the mammoth artifacts in the storeroom. So, Charlie, pack your ski clothes and other cold-weather gear!

USER 1
USER 2
USER 3

ON OUR WAY

Day 10

I can hardly believe I'm at the Museum of Zoology in St. Petersburg — one of Russia's largest natural history museums and one of more than 100 museums in the city.

The Museum of Zoology is the world headquarters for the study of mammoth remains. Its storerooms contain hundreds of specimens of preserved mammoth bone, chunks of mammoth hair, and pieces of soft tissue. The Beresovka mammoth — the most famous mammoth ever discovered — is displayed here.

Founded by Russian leader Peter the Great, St. Petersburg became the country's capital in 1712. (Moscow is the present-day capital of Russia.)

St. Petersburg is Russia's most European-looking city. Many of its huge palaces and ornate houses were converted into museums, theaters, and art galleries.

In 1900, the Beresovka mammoth was first found emerging from a frozen cliff.

The Beresovka mammoth

MAMMOTH ON DISPLAY 1904

In 1900, a hunter discovered the giant animal protruding from a frozen cliff along the Beresovka River. Imperial Academy zoologists Otto Herz and Eugen Pfizenmayer excavated the creature in 1901. They dissected the body on the spot and packed it into 27 cases. After a four-month journey across the frozen landscape by reindeer and horse sleigh, riverboat, and refrigerated train, it finally arrived at St. Petersburg on February 18, 1902. Although the mammoth delighted Russian leader Czar Nicholas II, his wife, Alexandra, found its smell overpowering. Preparators took two years to process the mammoth for display. The expedition cost 16,300 rubles — about $500 in U.S. dollars today!

The display of the Beresovka mammoth's skeleton was ready for display in 1904.

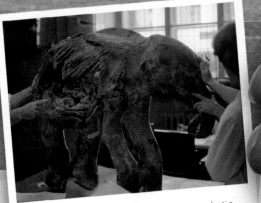

Scientists study the organs, muscles, brain, and other tissues of "Dima," the baby mammoth found in Siberia in 1977.

Dima lived less than one year. His heart is preserved for display.

The Beresovka mammoth

The Beresovka mammoth is displayed in the same position in which he was found — with his legs crumpled beneath him. This position made it impossible for him to get up.

About one-third of the model is covered with original skin and hair.

By the time it was found, most of the internal organs of the Beresovka mammoth had rotted away.

The mammoth was a male between 35 and 40 years old. Scientists think it died of asphyxiation (lack of oxygen). It still had food in its mouth, which suggests that it fell or became trapped while eating and died quickly.

A LONG JOURNEY

Day 14

Russia is much larger than I thought! It has taken Dr. Petronella and me several days to travel to the area where the mammoth pieces were found. The first stage of our journey was quick – a ninety-minute Aeroflot flight from St. Petersburg to Moscow.

St. Basil's cathedral in Moscow is a famous landmark.

After a meal of meatballs and pickled vegetables in Moscow's Yaroslavsky Railway Station, we began our eastward journey on the Trans-Siberian Railway to the town of Krasnoyarsk. The train ride took three days across wheat fields and through the Ural mountains. After the mountains came the coniferous forest called "taiga."

The last leg of our trip will be on a 1,243-mile (2,000-kilometer) steamboat ride on the Yenisei River.

Trans-Siberian railroad tracks stretch from Moscow to Vladivostok on the Pacific Ocean. It takes six days for the entire journey. A goat met our train at one of the stops!

A forest of pine and birch trees, called the taiga, covers the flat horizon.

The Arctic Circle is an imaginary line that marks the north end of Earth.

Dudinka, our destination, is also the mammoth site.

St. Petersburg

Moscow

We rode the Trans-Siberian train for three days.

Yenisei River

We spent five days traveling aboard the steamboat.

Krasnoyarsk

We boarded the Yenisei River steamboat in Krasnoyarsk, where the river is almost 1.5 miles (2 km) wide.

Day 15
We are traveling toward the Arctic Circle aboard the Yenisei River steamboat. The Yenisei completely cuts Siberia in half. I spend my time watching the soggy taiga forests go by. Our five-day trip includes food, but so far it's been only meatballs, meatballs, and more meatballs!

Day 18
We crossed the Arctic Circle two days ago and finally reached the small town of Dudinka. Now we see frozen tundra – flat, marshy plains with permanently frozen soil underneath – and few trees.

Herders tend their reindeer on the frozen winter tundra. In summer, the Sun never sets – even at midnight!

Day 19

As soon as we got off the boat at Dudinka, we met a gold miner who remembered the City Museum's expedition five years ago. He agreed to take us to the mining camp. There, we met Yuri, the guide who helped the museum team acquire the mammoth parts.

Yuri was reluctant to talk to us. He didn't really want to leave his gold mining work to take us to the mammoth remains. (Gold miners search for tiny pieces of gold in the riverbed grave. Every minute that Yuri is away from the river is lost income for him.)

Eventually, Yuri agreed to show us the place where the river was washing away its frozen bank. What an amazing sight — a half buried, thawing, and decaying mammoth sticking out of the ground!

Oh, but what an unbelievable stench!

Permafrost is a layer of frozen soil beneath the surface. This soil has probably been frozen for 40,000 years.

Global Positioning System (GPS) equipment pinpoints exact locations using satellite signals. It stores the data necessary to locate that precise location again in the future.

ANIMALS OF THE ARCTIC

Reindeer are the largest mammals in this part of the Arctic. In winter, reindeer grow shaggy hair and store layers of fat. Mammoths also survived these harsh conditions thousands of years ago thanks to their shaggy hair and fat layers. Reindeer scrape at the ground to loosen the snow and find the lichen on which they feed. Mammoths also dug for food in the snow using their tusks.

Yuri, a hard-working Siberian gold miner, was our reluctant guide.

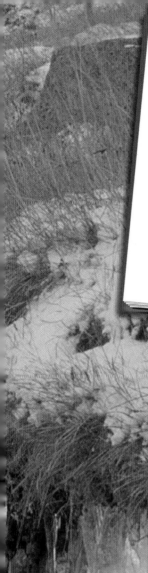

In some areas, the river thaws the land where it cuts into the permafrost.

We found a reddish, fibrous mass of mammoth hair.

Patches of exposed mammoth flesh have thawed and rotted.

A MAMMOTH UNDERTAKING

Two months later

We are back at the City Museum. Dr. Petronella says that the Arctic Circle weather is so brutal that we can only do research there for one or two months each year. She is convinced that we need a larger expedition to uncover what could be a mammoth herd.

The museum cannot afford such an expedition, so Dr. Petronella says we must look for private investors and corporate sponsorship from a big company. If the expedition is successful, the sponsors will get plenty of publicity.

Dr. Petronella is also contacting some film companies to see if they want to shoot a documentary (a factual television program) about the expedition. I think having a television film crew involved would really add to the excitement of our mammoth hunt!

marilyn's notes – Expedition Budget	
Food for twenty people for two months	$??
Cold-weather clothing for twenty people	$??
Flights, train, and steamboat fares	$??
Tents and camping equipment	$??
Rental of dogsleds or reindeer sleighs	$??
Dog/reindeer food	$??
Jackhammers (for breaking the ice)	$??
Seismological equipment	$??
Trucks to carry the specimens	$??
Storage facilities for the frozen specimens	$??
	$??

BOFFINBOX SCIENCE CHANNEL

We bring the latest scientific discoveries to the world — as they happen.

Dr. M. Petronella
c/o The City Museum

Dear Dr. Petronella,
We are very interested in your proposed expedition to excavate a frozen mammoth. If you allow our film crew to accompany you, we will cover the transportation costs for your personnel, storage costs for the specimens, and the use of our film crew and helicopter. As you may know, we made a documentary about the mammoth site in Hot Springs, South Dakota. That site was discovered in 1974, and so far, 52 skeletons of mammoths and many other different animals have been uncovered. These mammoths are the Columbian mammoth — a warm-climate mammoth species without much hair. We plan to make a film about the Siberian mammoths. We heard they will be excavated with flesh and hair intact!

Our film crew includes a cameraman, a sound person, and a reporter.

Mammoth Research in the United States

Scientists excavate Columbian mammoths, a North American mammoth species in Hot Springs, South Dakota.

Researchers believe the mammoths discovered food near a hot spring. They often tumbled down into the spring as they were eating. The mushy sides were too steep for the animals to climb back out, so they became trapped and died there.

From: The Legal office of Max J. Heidelmann, III
To: Dr. Marilyn Petronella, The City Museum
Subject: Funding of Siberian mammoth excavation

Dear Dr. Petronella,
My client, Mr. Max J. Heidelmann, III, is offering to fund your proposed mammoth expedition. Mr. Heidelmann enjoys supporting those who help expand humankind's frontiers of knowledge. He feels your endeavor is worthy of his attention and would like to accompany you on the expedition. Please submit a detailed breakdown of your anticipated expenses.

From: The Public Relations Office, Sugarybars, Inc.
Subject: Donation of food for Siberian expedition

Dear Dr. Petronella,
Please accept three cases of our Sugarybars ™. Our bars provide workers and athletes with an ideal energy supplement that's especially needed in freezing conditions.

BACK TO SIBERIA

At the dig site

We're back! It's the beginning of the summer and the digging season. Last time we traveled for days to reach this site, but this time we got here fast in a helicopter – courtesy of Boffinbox TV. (I have been told to say this at every opportunity). Our team includes volunteers, Mr. Heidelmann, III, the TV crew, Dr. Petronella, and me!

Word spread about our discovery, and many local people are here, too. The reindeer herders are very superstitious people – they believe that if you dig up a mammoth, you will die.

Ivory hunters have arrived as well. Mammoth ivory is very valuable and in great demand because the sale of elephant ivory was banned in 1989. Ivory hunters use high-pressure hoses to blast river water at the permafrost to thaw it. This frees the ivory but destroys the mammoth corpses. Some of the tusks we found last season have disappeared. Can the hunters be stopped?

Mammoth ivory sells for #200 per 2.2 pounds (1 kilogram) on the local market.

Ivory carvings for the tourist market are an important source of local income. Mammoth ivory is honey-colored, unlike elephant ivory, which is white.

I'm wrapped in layers of windproof and waterproof clothing.

Young children learn to interact with reindeer. The animals are used for food and clothing.

EARLY MAN & THE MAMMOTH

A Paleolithic hut found in Ukraine.

The mammoth was a great resource to Paleolithic humans who lived 45,000 – 10,000 years ago. Mammoths were trapped for their meat, skin, tusks, and bones. The shape and sturdiness of tusks made them ideal for building the curved walls of huts. This hut uses mammoth skulls, with a tusk in each, to form the entrance. Shoulder blades and limb bones surround the base. Curved mammoth ribs shape the roof. The hut is covered in mammoth skins.

The longest tusk ever recorded was 14 feet (4 m) long. An average male mammoth had tusks about 8 feet (2.5 m) long.

Day two of the dig

We struck a deal with the ivory hunters. They agreed to let us have one good mammoth specimen and will take what we leave behind. We gave them some gas for their trucks and a box of the Sugarybars, too. The ivory hunters consider them a luxury. We are sick of eating the bars!

We plan to study as much as we can at the site and collect plenty of samples of the frozen mud to take with us. The mud should contain plant remains that existed at the same time as our mammoth. These remains will tell us much about the mammoth's environment.

The carcass still has some flesh and internal organs. We should be able to find out from these how the mammoth lived. The thawed flesh and meat looks horrible and brown. Our cameraman bet me that he could eat some. He took a bite, then sputtered and spat it out. When he threw the meat to our team of huskies, even they wouldn't eat it!

SEISMIC READINGS REPORT

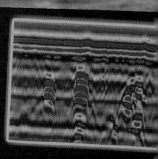

We can find whatever is in the ground using seismic equipment that geologists use for detecting earthquakes. We hit the ground with a hammer to send a shock wave through the ground, then detect the echoes with microphones. A seismic expert analyzes the computer readout of the echoes. Our survey suggests that there are a few mammoths buried in the frozen bank of the stream, and at least one good one is buried there.

SUGARY BARS

Huskies are perfectly adapted to life in this environment. Their protective double coat has an outer layer of smooth hairs and a thick woolly undercoat. Huskies work as a team to pull a loaded sled for long distances.

From: Charlie Smith
To: The Paleontology Department, The City Museum
Subject: Expedition report

Hi to all,

Today we have been using a scientific dating technique called electron spin resonance (ESR) dating. We hope this will tell us how long the mammoths have been buried in the mud. The fossilized carcasses will have received a steady dose of natural radiation from the soil surrounding them for the whole time they have been buried. This radiation becomes trapped in the fossils, in the form of electrons (minute particles that carry a negative electrical charge). We measure the amount of radiation coming from the mud and then measure how much radiation has built up in the fossils. From this, we can work out how long the fossils have been absorbing radiation, and, therefore, how long they have been in the ground.

We are also going to move one of the mammoths to the mammoth study center set up by the Russian authorities at Khatanga.

USER 1

USER 2

USER 3

A FLYING MAMMOTH

Two weeks later

We did it! We extracted an almost complete frozen mammoth in a block of permafrost. Russian law forbids the removal of mammoth remains from the country, so we must study it here. A helicopter will airlift the block containing the mammoth to the laboratory in Khatanga, 373 miles (600 km) away. The block weighs nearly 22 tons (20 tonnes).

We used a compressed-air jackhammer to dig out the solid block of permafrost. Then we used picks and shovels to chip away each side of the block until the mammoth's hair began to show. Finally, we put a steel frame beneath the block to support it.

The local reindeer herders were very superstitious and wanted us to appease the spirits by sacrificing a reindeer, but we satisfied them by throwing some coins into the hole where the mammoth had been.

The last team to fly a frozen mammoth to Khatanga by helicopter stuck a pair of tusks on it. It looked spectacular for the TV cameras but was not very scientific. It was also dangerous!

MAMMOTH GRAVEYARD FOUND

The skeletons of 156 individual mammoths, between 12,240 and 13,700 years old, have been found in the banks of the Berelekh River in Siberia. Since their discovery in 1970, scientists have been collecting the bones from the permanently frozen soil by thawing it out with hoses.

If we were only collecting the bones, we could have used hoses, too. Instead, we need to keep our specimen frozen to preserve the soft tissues.

MAMMOTH IN FLIGHT

OCTOBER 1999

Mammoth hunters in Siberia used a helicopter to transport a frozen mammoth from its icy tomb. Amazed crowds watched as the frozen block containing the Jarkov mammoth, complete with tusks sticking out, landed at the airfield of the small Arctic town of Khatanga.

🦣 🦣 🦣 🦣 🦣 🦣 🦣 🦣 🦣 🦣 🦣

From: The Cryogenics Laboratory
To: Max J. Heidelmann, c/o Charlie Smith

Dear Max,
The cryogenic equipment is ready. Bring whatever samples you can extract from the frozen mammoth. We shall try to sequence the DNA for your first steps in the experiment to clone the mammoth someday.

From: Charlie Smith
To: Dr. Marilyn Petronella

Dear Dr. Petronella,
Take a look at the e-mail that just arrived for Mr. Heidelmann! DNA? Cloning? I'm not sure I understand all this. I know they used DNA to clone dinosaurs in the book and film *Jurassic Park*, but what is DNA exactly? Could Mr. Heidelmann actually re-create an extinct animal? What should we do?

USER 1

USER 2

USER 3

AT THE STUDY CENTER

Scientist at work!

When Dr. Petronella found out that Mr. Heidelmann's real reason for accompanying us was to try to clone a mammoth, I thought she would be furious. Instead, she is amused. Dr. Petronella doesn't think a mammoth will ever be cloned, but she regards Mr. Heidelmann's plan as a legitimate science research project and an offshoot of our own research.

We are now studying the mammoth in detail. The Khatanga study center is a former nickel mine, located deep in the frozen rocks. Now it's a refrigerated storeroom for thousands of frozen mammoth parts and tusks. The temperature inside is 14° Fahrenheit (- 10° Celsius), about the same temperature as the exposed tundra. Nothing thaws here unless we want it to.

The first piece of the mammoth to be defrosted is a reddish-brown hank of hair 35 inches (90 centimeters) long. It may have changed color after death.

Just like tree rings, growth lines in a cross-section of mammoth tusk may tell us the age of the animal when it died.

We use an ordinary hairdryer to defrost our mammoth a little at a time. We can then study each piece in detail.

Scientists wear sterile anticontamination suits, gloves, and masks over their cold-weather gear when handling the frozen remains. These steps prevent contamination of the mammoth specimens.

Dr. Petronella says that chemical analyses of the hair may eventually reveal if the mammoths had black coats just like the modern musk ox.

DNA (deoxyribonucleic acid) and Cloning
Frequently Asked Questions

What is deoxyribonucleic acid (DNA)?
All living things are made from cells. Each cell is controlled by a nucleus. Inside the nucleus are chromosomes, which contain DNA. A specific pattern of DNA linkage is called a gene; genes carry the instructions for making a copy of that animal or plant.

What is cloning?
Cloning is the creation of an animal or plant that is an exact genetic replica of its parent.

How could an extinct animal like a mammoth be cloned?
Remove the egg cell from the womb of a modern, female Asian elephant and destroy the cell's nucleus. Replace the original nucleus with a complete and undamaged nucleus from a frozen mammoth cell containing mammoth DNA (instructions for the cells to grow into a mammoth). Implant the special egg cell into the elephant's uterus. The elephant should give birth to a mammoth.

If DNA is found, it may help tell us about the health of the mammoth. It will also help determine the genetic relationship between mammoths and modern-day elephants.

I don't think this will ever work! DNA begins to deteriorate immediately after death. You need high-quality DNA to create a healthy offspring. So let Mr. Heidelmann have his specimens.
— someday scientists might get it right!

marilyn P

Back home

Although we could not remove the whole mammoth from Russia, we were allowed to bring back many of our samples to the City Museum. It's amazing just how much information we can get from individual pieces of the body as well as from the mud in which the mammoth was buried.

From the shape of its pelvis, we know that our mammoth was male. The state of the molar tooth and the rings in the tusk show that he was elderly — maybe forty years old. Mammoths could live to about age sixty.

We compared the amount of natural radiation absorbed by his tooth enamel and dentin with the radiation that we measured at the site. We determined that our mammoth died about 12,000 years ago. If we want further evidence of what our mammoth looked like, we can refer to eyewitness accounts. Our final clues are in France.

Like modern elephants, mammoths went through seven sets of teeth in their lifetime. Scientists think this tooth is from our mammoth's final set.

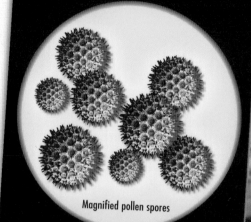

The Mammoth's Last Meal
Report from
the City Museum Botany Department

Pollen and spores from the mammoth's stomach contents as well as the mud in which it was buried are distinctive enough to identify the plant species it ate. Its stomach held sedges, mosses, grasses, and dwarf willows. The mammoth lived on open grasslands.

Magnified pollen spores

MAMMOTH CAVE PAINTINGS
Mammoth paintings on cave walls tell us that Paleolithic people at the end of the Ice Age shared their world with these behemoths. This cave painting of a shaggy mammoth, at Pech Merle in France, is part of a famous Paleolithic artwork called the "Black Frieze." The 1.25-mile- (2-km-) long cave complex contains images of mammoths, horses, bison, and even some 10,000-year-old human footprints.

MAMMOTH IVORY CARVING
This mammoth made from tusk ivory was probably carved about 20,000 years ago. The craftsperson could have actually watched live mammoths as he or she worked.

Cave paintings and carvings confirm that mammoths had shaggy hair to keep them warm. The hump on the shoulders probably contained fat to keep the mammoth nourished through the harsh winter.

Opening day

At last we can present our mammoth to the City Museum visitors. The centerpiece of the display is a magnificent animatronic replica of the mammoth. We took precise measurements of the skeleton back in Khatanga and estimated the volume of muscle that the mammoth had in life. Workers then built this accurate, full-sized, fiberglass replica. The parts of the pelt (hair-covered skin) that we were allowed to bring back are attached to the model, and the rest of the coat is re-created from nylon fibers. The tusks are based on the measurements of the originals and made from lightweight plastic. We have also been able to display the teeth, the stomach contents, and some of the internal organs. It is important that visitors see the original material, and that original material is also kept available for scientific research. The expedition increased our knowledge and understanding of woolly mammoths!

Here I am visiting our mammoth at the animatronics workshop. It can move its head from side to side and reach out to the crowds with its huge trunk. Inside the body, a central computer and other complicated electronics control its movements. It would have been amazing to clone a mammoth and bring it back to life, but at least I can visit the City Museum anytime to see my very own Ice Age giant in action!

10 ft (3 m)

6.5 ft (2m)

3.3 ft (1m)

**THE CITY MUSEUM
MAMMOTH**

This display sponsored by
Boffinbox Science Channel *and*
Max J. Heidelmann, III.

GLOSSARY

African elephant: an elephant species native to Africa with large ears, two "lips" on its trunk, and three toenails on its hind feet. Males and females both grow tusks.

animatronic: a model or puppet that moves electronically.

Arctic Circle: an imaginary line at 66.5 degrees north latitude that surrounds the North Pole. Here, in summer, the Sun never sets, and in winter, the Sun never rises.

Asian elephant: an elephant species native to Asia with small ears, one "lip" on its trunk, a bulging forehead, and four toenails on its hind feet. Only males grow tusks.

asphyxiation: to die by suffocation.

behemoth: something that is very enormous.

carcass: a dead animal body.

cell: the smallest structural unit of living matter capable of independent function.

climate: the average weather conditions in a region over a period of years, including temperature and amount of rainfall.

clone: to produce a new plant or animal that is genetically identical to its parent.

coniferous: a tree or shrub that produces cones. It usually remains green year-round.

decay: to rot or decompose because of the action of bacteria or fungi.

DNA (deoxyribonucleic acid): the long-stranded molecule found within the nucleus of a living cell. The pattern of links in the strand of DNA forms the genes.

dwarf: a smaller than normal form of an animal or a plant.

Electron Spin Resonance (ESR) dating: an experimental method of dating materials such as fossils, bones, or teeth that measures the change in the absorption of energy in a magnetic field. Over time, buried specimens absorb radiation from the soil around them. The ESR date of the specimen is compared with the ESR date of the surrounding soil to calculate how long the specimen has been buried.

environment: the area, terrain, climate, and any other external factors that affect the lives of plants and animals.

Eocene: an epoch of the Tertiary period of geological time, stretching from 55 to 35 million years ago.

erosion: a gradual wearing away by wind, water, ice, or repeated contact with a foreign substance.

ethnographer: someone who studies people and their cultures.

evolve: to change and develop over a period of time.

excavate: to remove the top layer to expose what's underneath.

extinct: no longer in existence.

fossil: the remains of once-living things — or even footprints — preserved in rock.

genes: parts of living cells that contain the instructions for determining what that living thing will be like and what features it will have throughout its life.

glacier: a large mass of ice that moves slowly down a valley or across a continent, melting at one end and being replenished by snow at the other.

Global Positioning System (GPS): an electronic navigational system that uses signals from 24 satellites in geosynchronous orbit to pinpoint an exact location anywhere on Earth.

Ice Age: a period of time when climates were much colder than they are now.

jackhammer: a large mechanical drill that is used for breaking up solid surfaces.

lichen: a plantlike partnership between a fungus and an alga. Lichen grow on a variety of surfaces, such as rocks or tree trunks.

mammoth: very large, extinct elephant-like animals with long tusks.

Miocene: an epoch of the Tertiary period of geological time, stretching from 23 to 5 million years ago.

molar: a grinding tooth at the back of the jaw.

nucleus: the central part of a living cell, containing DNA with coded segments known as genes that determine reproduction and growth.

Oligocene: an epoch of the Tertiary period of geological time, stretching from 35 to 23 million years ago.

Paleolithic: of the earliest part of the Stone Age, from about 750,000 to 15,000 years ago.

paleontologist: someone who studies fossils to find out about animals and plants that lived in prehistoric times.

permafrost: a layer of permanently frozen soil found beneath the surface of many cold areas.

Pleistocene: an epoch of the Quaternary period of geological time, stretching from 1.6 million to 10,000 years ago.

pollen: particles that the male part of a flower releases to fertilize the female part of flowers.

Quaternary: a period of geological time lasting from about 1.8 million years ago to the present day. The first humans appeared during the Quaternary period.

radiation: energy radiated from a source in the form of waves or particles.

replica: an accurate reproduction, copy, or model of a plant, animal, or thing.

sedges: tufted marsh plants.

seismic: relating to vibrations and Earth movements.

species: a particular kind of animal or plant.

specimen: a sample of something used for scientific study.

spore: the tiny part of a plant that takes part in fertilization. A pollen grain is a kind of spore.

taiga: the vast stretch of coniferous forest that reaches across northern Asia close to the Arctic Circle.

Tertiary: a period of geological time lasting from about 65 to 1.8 million years ago. It was marked by the dominance of mammals and the evolution of modern-day plants.

tissue: the substance, such as skin and muscle, that makes up the parts of a living creature.

tundra: a boggy landscape of low-growing plants that forms over permafrost.

yearling: an animal that is at least one year — but not more than two years — old.

zoology: the study of animals and their lives.

MORE INFORMATION

BOOKS

The Fate of the Mammoth: Fossils, Myth, and History. Claudine Cohen (University of Chicago Press)

Ice Age Mammoth: Will This Ancient Giant Come Back to Life? Barbara Hehner (Crown)

Mammoth: Gone Forever. Rupert Matthews (Heinemann)

Mammoths: Ice-Age Giants. Discovery! (series). Larry D. Agenbroad (Lerner)

Who Are You Calling a Woolly Mammoth?: Prehistoric America. America's Horrible Histories, 1 (series). Elizabeth Levy (Scholastic)

Wild and Woolly Mammoths. Aliki (HarperCollins)

A Woolly Mammoth Journey. Debbie S. Miller (Little, Brown & Co.)

WEB SITES

www.mammothsite.com
Scroll to the links for kids.

www.ktca.org/newtons/11/prmfrost.html
Learn about permafrost.

arts.uwaterloo.ca/ANTHRO/rwpark/ArcticArchStuff/Fieldwork.html
Includes images and brief text describing what it takes to carry out research where the ground is always frozen.

VIDEOS

Cousteau: Voyage to the Edge of the World — An Arctic Adventure. (United American Video)

Raising the Mammoth. (Artisan Entertainment)

Time Machine: Arctic Tomb. (A & E Home Video)

INDEX